LONGMAN ORIGINALS Stage Four
Series editor: Robert O'Neill

THE MAN WHO MADE

Diamonds

Mandy Loader

Illustrations by Mike Bell

LONGMAN

Addison Wesley Longman Limited,
Edinburgh Gate, Harlow,
Essex CM20 2JE, England
and Associated Companies throughout the world

First published 1995
Second impression 1996

Set in 11/13pt Melior, Adobe/Linotype (postscript)
Produced by Longman Singapore Publishers Pte Ltd
Printed in Singapore

ISBN 0 582 08144 0

Contents

CHAPTER ONE
Diamonds can destroy lives

London, September 1963...
It was a warm, sunny afternoon, and the streets were full of young people. They were talking and laughing. Everybody seemed to be in a holiday mood. All except one young man. He was sitting alone at a table just outside a small restaurant in the theatre district. He looked very serious. He was tall and good-looking, but very pale. It was the paleness of someone who lived and worked in dark rooms.

Two young women were sitting at the next table. They looked at the young man and then at each other. One of the young women looked back at him again, but the young man didn't notice her. He was reading a newspaper. A waiter came out of the restaurant and walked towards the young man's table.

"*Buongiorno, signor Rogers.* Do you want the same pizza you always have?" he asked

"Hello, Giorgio. Yes, the one with mushrooms," the young man said. He did not look at the waiter when he spoke. He was still reading the newspaper. The waiter looked at it, too.

"You're reading that article about diamonds, aren't you?"

The young man looked up at the waiter.

"Yes, I am."

"Do you believe what the article says? Can it be true?"

"I don't know, Giorgio. I've read articles like this before. And they weren't true."

"So you don't believe this article, then?"

"I didn't say that, Giorgio. I just don't know."

A few minutes later, the waiter came back with the pizza. The young man was still looking at the newspaper article.

"You know," the waiter said, "in the evening people come

to our restaurant after the opera or the theatre. Sometimes they wear their very best clothes and jewellery. Yesterday evening, I saw a woman with a very beautiful diamond around her neck. It wasn't a very big diamond, but – "

The young man looked up from his newspaper.

"What was it like?" he asked.

"Well, signor Rogers, to me diamonds are all the same colour – white. But this diamond was different. It wasn't white but blue... well... you know, very light blue. Like the colour of the sky in Sicily early in the morning."

A strange look came over the young man's face.

"Perhaps it came from the Bonington mine in South Africa. Bonington diamonds are a very special kind of blue. And they're usually a little smaller than diamonds from the De Beers mines. Yes, perhaps it was a Bonington diamond."

When he said the name, he looked at the newspaper again.

"How much does a diamond like that cost, signor Rogers?" the waiter asked

"A lot, Giorgio. Even small diamonds like that are very expensive – but perhaps they won't be so expensive much longer – not if this article is correct."

The waiter did not move from the young man's table. But the young man was still staring at the newspaper. Then Georgio remembered a story about another customer at the restaurant.

"I knew a woman once who had some beautiful diamond jewellery. She came to this restaurant very often. Then she stopped coming. Later I found out that someone had stolen all her diamonds. When that happened, the woman had a heart attack and died. Just imagine! She loved those diamonds more than anything – and when they were stolen, the shock killed her."

"Yes, I know, Giorgio. People lie and steal for diamonds. Diamonds are very beautiful but they can destroy people's lives," the young man said without looking up from the newspaper.

Peter Rogers finished his pizza, walked to the edge of the street and got into a taxi. It was much cheaper and just as fast to take the Underground to where he wanted to go. But Peter Rogers hated being below ground.

The taxi driver was smoking.

"Where to?" he asked without taking the cigarette from his mouth. The words came out in a cloud of smoke.

"Hatton Garden."

The driver knew the street well. It was the centre of London's diamond industry. Diamond sellers, buyers and cutters worked in Hatton Garden. Millions of pounds of jewels were bought and sold there every day.

"Have you seen the news about that company in South Africa?" the driver asked.

"Yes."

"Funny old world, isn't it? If the news is true, I'll be able to get a diamond necklace for the wife now."

Peter said nothing. The taxi took him to a long, narrow street and stopped in front of a low, two-storey building with a green door. He pressed a bell and waited. Then he knocked on the door loudly. There was one small window on the ground floor and there were three larger windows on the floor above. They all had heavy steel bars across them.

He rang the bell and knocked again. There was a small hole in the door and he knew that someone was there, looking through it.

"Barbara, it's me. Hurry up. Open the door," he shouted.

There was a kind of 'clang', like the sound of prison bars being opened. Finally, the door swung back. A young woman with dark hair was standing there.

"I didn't hear you," she said.

He went through the door and waited while the young woman locked and bolted it. Then they went through another steel door into a small office.

"I was typing a letter. I had those on," she said, pointing to a pair of headphones next to the recording machine on her desk.

"Is Mr Goodman in?" he asked, looking around the office.

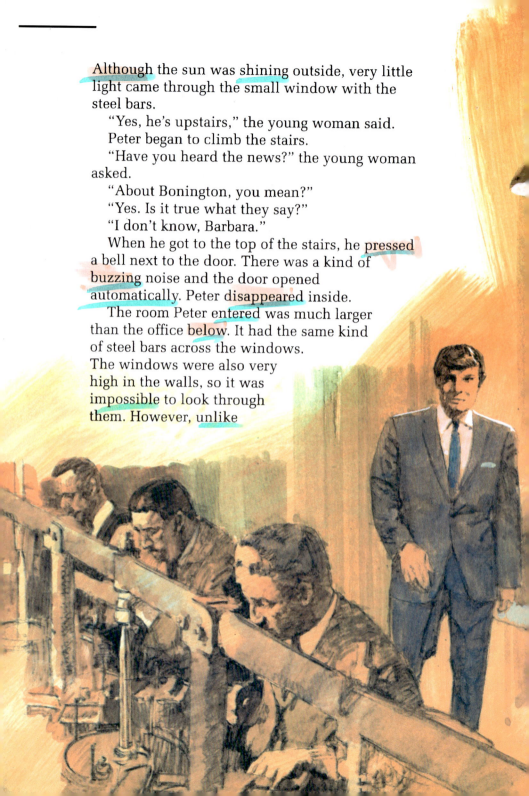

Although the sun was shining outside, very little light came through the small window with the steel bars.

"Yes, he's upstairs," the young woman said.

Peter began to climb the stairs.

"Have you heard the news?" the young woman asked.

"About Bonington, you mean?"

"Yes. Is it true what they say?"

"I don't know, Barbara."

When he got to the top of the stairs, he pressed a bell next to the door. There was a kind of buzzing noise and the door opened automatically. Peter disappeared inside.

The room Peter entered was much larger than the office below. It had the same kind of steel bars across the windows. The windows were also very high in the walls, so it was impossible to look through them. However, unlike the office, there were bright working lamps hanging from the high ceiling, and the room was very busy. Several different types of machines were running and the workers were bent over their machines under the lights. They were all wearing work-clothes and they didn't look up as Peter went into the room. Peter walked quickly past them and knocked on a door at the far end of the room. He heard Goodman's voice call out, "Is that you, Peter? Come in."

Peter opened the heavy door and went into a small, dark room. It was square, like a box, and rather small. A bright lamp was shining in the darkness. It did not look like an important company director's office, but it was.

An old man with a grey beard in an old-fashioned black suit was sitting at the old wooden desk in the lamplight. He was wearing a jeweller's eye-glass. There were some small but very bright diamonds on a black cloth in front of him.

"Peter. Good afternoon. Sit down," he said.

The old man took the eye-glass off and carefully placed it next to the diamonds on the black cloth. Then he put on a pair of thick glasses and stood up to welcome Peter.

"Look at them. Just think how long it took for each one to form," the old man said, pointing to the diamonds.

Peter noticed a newspaper on the desk next to the diamonds. The old man pointed to it. On the front page, there was a picture of a smiling man in a white coat. It was the same newspaper Peter had been reading in the restaurant.

"And now they say it's possible to make synthetic diamonds which are just as good as natural ones."

"Yes, I know. I've read the article, too," Peter said.

All the newspapers that day had articles about a company called Bonington in South Africa. Some of the world's finest natural diamonds had come from the company's mine. The newspapers said that one of Bonington's directors, Professor Alan Hartwell had invented a machine that could make gemstone diamonds. Gemstone diamonds were the best type of natural diamonds, very different from the diamonds that were used in industry.

"Do you know this Professor Hartwell?" Peter asked and pointed to the picture of the smiling man in the white coat.

"Yes, of course I do. He's Bonington's technical director."

"What do you think of him?"

"Everyone says he's a brilliant scientist."

"Well, perhaps he's made a mistake," Peter said.

The old man looked at him through his thick glasses.

"A mistake? No, I don't think so. A man like Professor Hartwell doesn't make mistakes. Not mistakes like this."

For a moment, both men were silent. The only sounds in the room came through the heavy door from the workroom outside and from an old clock above one of the safes.

"Let me put these diamonds back in the safe," he said.

He counted the diamonds one by one, and put them into small bags made of black cloth. Then he pushed back his chair and got to his feet. He was slow and careful in everything he did. There were three safes behind him, standing like soldiers on parade. He took out some heavy keys from his pocket and unlocked the door of the third safe. Then he bent down to open a second door with a special combination lock.

"What will happen to the price of natural diamonds?" Peter asked.

Goodman did not answer. He seemed to be deep in thought as he quietly put the diamonds back in the safe. He locked the two doors of the safe and then came back to his desk. He stared at the newspaper again.

"The article says that Bonington has just announced a plan to build a large, completely new factory with the most modern technology. Hartwell says he can make five thousand diamonds of gemstone quality a day. They say they can sell them at less than half the price of natural diamonds. If that's true, it will of course be a disaster for companies like us. We've invested large sums of money in natural diamonds. But who will want them if synthetic gemstones are just as good and cost only half as much?"

CHAPTER TWO
Breaking diamonds

Goodman and Son, the company Peter Rogers worked for, was very important in London's diamond business. Peter was in charge of publicity and information and often worked very late at nights.

Peter was extremely busy the following week. Every day there was another article in the newspapers about the new synthetic diamonds. Some of the articles said the price of natural diamonds would fall by as much as fifty per cent. One of the articles even said that natural gemstones would soon be almost worthless.

The price of shares in Bonington went higher and higher on the stock market every day. The price of shares in the companies that produced natural diamonds fell.

Mr Goodman spent hours and hours on the phone talking to friends and other people in the diamond business in New York, Antwerp, Paris, Sydney and other cities.

One afternoon later that week, Peter was sitting with Mr Goodman when the phone rang. It was Barbara, the dark-haired young woman who worked downstairs.

"Mr Goodman. I'm looking for Peter. He's not in his office. Is he with you?"

"Yes. Why?"

"There's a group of students here. They're waiting for him."

"Oh, no! I'd forgotten them," Peter said to Goodman. He sometimes took groups of interested people through the workshop and explained what was happening. It was part of his job. He stood up and went to the door.

"Just a moment, Peter."

Peter stopped and looked back at the old man.

"Say as little as possible about these new synthetic diamonds."

"But they've probably seen some of the articles in the newspapers. They'll almost certainly ask me questions about them."

The old man thought for a second.

"In that case, tell them that we have nothing to say… for the moment."

Peter took a white coat from the small changing room on the first floor and ran down the stairs to the reception area. Twelve university students were waiting there.

"Good afternoon, everyone. My name is Peter Rogers. I'm going to show you around the workrooms and tell you the fascinating story of diamonds and what we do to them here. We'll go to the cutting room first. Come this way, please," Peter said quickly.

He took the group up the stairs. They followed him like sheep.

"Good," he thought. "I don't think I'm going to have any trouble with this group."

Then he noticed a young woman standing at the back of the group. She was a little older than the other students. She was wearing a black leather jacket and denim jeans. She was pointing to a newspaper in her hand and whispering to another student.

The group crowded into the first workroom.

"This is the cutting room," Peter said.

The noise of machines filled the room. The people working at the machines were handling dark, rough stones. The students looked disappointed.

"Are these things really diamonds?" one of them asked.

"They will be, but they have to be broken, cut and polished first," Peter answered.

"Broken? I thought diamonds were the hardest things in the world," another student at the front of the group said.

Peter looked at the back of the group. The woman in the leather jacket was still reading the newspaper. Peter looked back at the student who had just asked the question.

"It depends what you mean by 'hard'. Diamonds are very hard when you use them for cutting metal or stone. But they can be broken quite easily if you hit them in a certain way and at a certain point. They can also be broken if you drop them. That's why we always hold large diamonds very carefully," he explained.

"The machines over there are saws. We use them to cut the diamonds. We use a mixture of diamond powder and olive oil on the saws," he continued, pointing to some other machines.

All the students looked bored. One of them in the middle of the group yawned.

"Let's go to the grinding room now," Peter shouted.

The students followed him as he took them to another, much smaller workroom. It was also much quieter than the first room. Instead of the loud sounds that the saws and cutting machines had made, there was only a low hum. Ten men were sitting around a table, working busily.

"As I told you, first the stones have to be broken and cut. Then we have to grind them – and this is what these men are doing."

One of the students stepped nearer the men at the table. The student stared at the workmen's hands and then back at Peter. There was a strange look of disgust and fascination on his face.

"Why are the hands of those men so... so...," he began in a low whisper.

"Do you mean what does this work do to the hands of the men who have to grind the stones?" Peter said loudly.

Even the student who had yawned looked a little less sleepy. Peter walked over to one of the men.

"George. Show these students your right hand."

The students couldn't see George's face, but Peter could. George winked at Peter and put down the diamonds he was holding. Then he turned to the students and proudly held up his right hand. It didn't look like a human hand. It looked more like the claw of a very large bird. The first and second fingers were very large and bent. The thumb was also very large and seemed to be bent permanently. The skin was very hard and shiny – more like a shell than skin. George stood up and walked over the students. They all moved backwards.

"This is what happens to your hand if you work with diamonds for a few years," George said. Then he turned and walked back to the worktable. His back was turned to the students again.

Peter smiled again at George and the other men at the table. None of the students looked sleepy any more. He held the door open as the students walked out. Before he followed them, he turned back to the men at the table.

"Thanks, George. That really woke them up," he whispered. George and the other men at the table laughed.

Peter turned back to the students. He suddenly felt very tired.

"Well, I hope you've enjoyed the tour," he said, and began walking towards the outer door.

The young woman in the leather jacket suddenly raised her hand.

"Yes?" Peter asked, without enthusiasm.

"Have you seen this article about man-made diamonds?" she asked, and held up the newspaper.

"No, I don't think I have. Now, unless you have any questions, we –"

She began speaking again before he could finish.

"The article says that a company in South Africa plans to make five thousand synthetic gemstones a day. What do you think about that?"

"No comment, I'm afraid."

"What? You mean you don't read the papers?"

"Yes, I read the papers," Peter said quietly.

She waited for him to go on. But Peter turned and began leading the students towards the outer door.

"Well, surely then you know what they're saying? Are you telling us you have no opinion at all about these reports?"

Several students laughed.

"Of course I have an opinion!" Peter said loudly. This student was beginning to annoy him.

"Well? Do you believe it's possible to make diamonds?"

Peter took a deep breath and looked at the young woman. He tried to speak calmly.

"Yes, it's possible to make diamonds. They've been doing it for the last five years. But these are industrial diamonds. They're used for cutting and other purposes. "

"But what about larger stones – gemstones?" she asked.

"No, you can't make gemstones."

"Why not? You say there's already a technique to make industrial diamonds."

"Yes, there is. But gemstones are much bigger than industrial diamonds. Nobody has ever produced a synthetic diamond of gemstone quality. A lot of people have tried, but nobody has succeeded."

"But this article says that Professor... Professor..." She looked back at the newspaper.

"Hartwell. Professor Hartwell," Peter said.

"Yes. Hartwell. The article says that his synthetic diamonds are just as good and as big as natural gemstones."

There was a silence in the room. All the students were watching Peter.

"There was a Scottish chemist once who said he could make diamonds. They were very small but they were still diamonds. That was in 1880. In 1943, those diamonds were X-rayed. Guess what they found?" he asked.

The young woman didn't answer. Peter continued.

"They found that they weren't synthetic diamonds at all. They were real. Some people think the Scottish chemist used tiny pieces of natural diamonds to make them. In other words, he was a fraud."

"Doesn't your company buy diamonds from Bonington?" the young woman asked.

"Yes."

"Does that mean your company is working with frauds?" she suddenly demanded.

Again, three or four students laughed. The young woman smiled at them quickly.

Peter remembered what Mr Goodman had told him earlier.

He looked at his watch and then back at the group of students.

"We have nothing to say about this at the moment. Now, you'll have to excuse me. I have work to do," he answered quietly.

He could see Barbara, the secretary, standing at the back of the group. There was a very worried look on her face.

"Barbara. Please show these students out," he said. Then he turned to the students again and thanked them for coming.

"Not such a boring afternoon, after all," one of them said to another as they left. The young woman in the leather jacket was smiling. She clearly felt that she had won the argument.

Barbara locked and bolted the front door and turned to Peter.

"What's all this about frauds? What's it got to do with Bonington's?" she asked.

Peter began to answer but the telephone suddenly rang. Barbara answered it.

There was a short pause. Then Barbara spoke to Mr Goodman.

"There's a call for you – from South Africa."

Peter hurried up to Goodman's office. He opened the door without knocking. Goodman had the phone in his hand. He waved at Peter, as if to say, "Come in." Peter sat down on the chair in front of the desk.

"What do you mean? When?" Goodman said. The old man looked worried – very worried.

"But... who would do such a thing?" he shouted.

CHAPTER THREE
The Demon King

Goodman listened for a few more moments. Then he said, "Stephanie, Peter Rogers is here with me. I'd like to discuss this with him. I'll phone you again in an hour or so."

He hung up and stared at Peter.

"That was Stephanie Powers," Goodman said.

Peter remembered the name. She was the attractive young woman who had come to London last summer with her father, the financial director of Bonington's. She had been working for the company at that time but had recently started a university course in Cape Town. He also remembered her eyes. They were very, very blue.

"What did she say?" Peter asked.

Goodman did not answer him. He was shaking his head.

"Mr Goodman. Please. Tell me. What did she say?"

Goodman covered his eyes for a moment and then looked up at Peter.

"Stephanie's father disappeared the day before yesterday. They say he was kidnapped by a gang of terrorists."

Peter could hardly believe his ears.

"Kidnapped? When?"

"Yesterday."

Peter stood up. He walked around the room for a minute, thinking.

"There's something wrong with all this, Mr Goodman. First Bonington makes this announcement. Then Stephanie's father, the financial director, disappears."

Goodman said nothing.

"Do you know Bonington very well?" Peter asked.

"I've known him for a long time, if that's what you mean."

"Doesn't that mean you know him well?"

"No. I don't think Bonington is the kind of man anyone knows very well."

"Do you trust him?"

Goodman seemed to be thinking. Peter felt that the old man did not want to answer the question.

"I've done business with him for a long time. He's always been honest with me," he said after a moment's silence.

Goodman looked at Peter. For a moment Peter was afraid that the old man was not going to say anything more. Again, he seemed to be thinking. Then he spoke again.

"You know, it's strange but I spoke to Stephanie's father only a short time before I heard about these new synthetic diamonds. He was very worried," he finally said.

"Worried? About what?"

"He didn't tell me. I had the feeling that he wanted to, but for some reason he didn't."

Peter took a step closer to Goodman's desk.

"Do you think there's a connection between that and his kidnapping? I mean, perhaps he knew something that Bonington didn't want anyone else to know?"

Goodman shook his head. He looked like a man who had just had a bad dream.

"I can't say. I just don't know."

Goodman closed his mouth tightly. Peter sat down and waited. But the old man had said all he wanted to say. He was looking up at the ceiling.

"Mr Goodman. Send me to South Africa," Peter said.

Goodman didn't seem to hear. He was still staring at the ceiling, with a far-away look in his eye. Peter looked up at the ceiling, too. He saw a fly there. It was caught in a spider's web.

"All my friends in the diamond trade here in London – and in Antwerp and New York – will probably go out of business," Goodman said slowly, still looking at the fly in the spider's web. The spider was moving slowly towards the fly.

"I don't believe the story. I think Hartwell is a fraud," Peter said in a loud voice.

The old man still didn't seem to hear. There was the same far-away look in his eyes.

"Send me to South Africa," Peter said again.

There was a loud buzzing noise from the fly. Peter looked at it again. The spider suddenly moved towards the fly very quickly. The buzzing noise stopped. Goodman looked back at Peter again.

"We're as helpless as that fly. You can't stop progress. Times change. We have to change with them," he said slowly.

"But Mr Goodman, if the story is true, all the diamond mines will close. Nobody will want to dig in the earth if good diamonds of gemstone quality can be made in a factory."

Peter knew what the old man was going to do next. He always did it when he was facing a very serious problem. Goodman stood up and walked over to the heaviest of all the safes. He pulled out his keys again and began to unlock the safe. Peter went on talking

"And what about the stones themselves? There won't be any great diamonds any more. No Tiffany Yellows."

The old man bent down and opened the second door of the safe. Peter wasn't sure if he was listening. Peter raised his voice.

"No Tiger Eyes. No Cullinan stones. Factory diamonds won't have the character of natural diamonds. "

Goodman took out a small cloth bag. Then he closed and locked the two doors of the safe and brought the bag back to the desk.

"Yes," he said to Peter, as he put the bag gently on his desk. "You're quite right. Man-made diamonds will all be the same. Nothing like these."

He opened the bag, which Peter knew contained the 'Goodman collection' – wonderful diamonds that the Goodman family had collected over a period of a hundred years. The old man took out the stones and placed them carefully on his desk. Then he moved the lamp on his desk so that the light shone down onto the stones.

The diamonds had so many shapes, sizes and colours! One of them had a very rare, bluish colour. Another was dark brown. There was also a bright yellow stone and several that were pink or deep, blood red. Others were pure white.

Peter was afraid that he would never get the old man's attention. He tried again.

"Mr Goodman. Please send me to Kimberley. Let me talk to Hartwell and Bonington. Perhaps I can find out what really happened to Stephanie's father."

Goodman picked up one of the stones. It was very large and oval-shaped.

"The Eugenie Stone. The diamond of empresses. It was Napoleon III's wedding gift to his beautiful bride, Eugenie. Before that it belonged to Catherine II of Russia."

Peter had heard Goodman talk like this before. He could go on for hours.

The old man turned the diamond over in his hand. It caught the light in the dark room and reflected it brilliantly.

"Look how it flashes. They say it has a heart of pure fire inside. It has moods and different colours. Sometimes it's brilliant, like the full moon Sometimes it's cloudy, like the sky on a stormy day."

Goodman put the beautiful diamond back on the desk and picked up another.

"And this is the Regent diamond. A perfect, brilliant stone. It weighed 800 carats when it was discovered. Louis XIV of France wore this stone in his crown at his coronation in 1722."

He paused but did not take his eyes off the diamond.

"It was stolen during the French Revolution and then it

was given to Napoleon. Napoleon sold it and used the money to buy food for his soldiers. This is a stone of kings and emperors. A pure fire burns in it. But it often brings disaster to those who own it."

The old man seemed to be in another world. Peter knew there was only one way he could get his attention. Perhaps he could use the story of the stone that Goodman called the Star Gazer. It was next to Goodman's left hand.

"Mr Goodman. What about the Star Gazer? Look at the Star Gazer, Mr Goodman."

Instead, Goodman picked up the stone next to his right hand.

"This is the Star of Africa," he said slowly.

"No, not the Star of Africa. The Star Gazer, Mr Goodman."

Again, Goodman didn't seem to hear.

"My grandfather bought this stone from a boy who had found it while looking after his father's sheep. The boy didn't want to want to sell the stone for money, so my grandfather paid the boy five hundred sheep, ten oxen and a horse. The boy was very happy with the deal and so was my grandfather. He sold the stone for £11,000 in London in 1880 and I bought it again in 1920 for £20,000."

"But what about the Star Gazer? Look at it. What do you see?" Peter said softly.

At last, Goodman looked up at Peter.

"You once told me that when you look into the Star Gazer, you have a clear picture of the future. Look into it now, Mr Goodman. Can you see what will happen to this company and to all the other companies that deal in natural diamonds? Can you see how many people will lose their jobs?"

The only sound in the room was the clock, ticking as each second went by.

The old man slowly picked up the Star Gazer and looked into it. It was a large, pure white stone.

"Tell me what you see, Mr Goodman."

Goodman put the stone down.

"Nothing. Today I can see nothing," the old man said.

"That's why you must send me to South Africa. You can't see anything in the stone because the future is uncertain. Perhaps I can find out if Hartwell's story is really true."

Goodman shook his head.

"I was just like you when I was younger. I was a fighter. I was impatient."

He put the stones back in the bag.

"Will you send me to South Africa?" Peter asked.

The old man got up slowly and took the bag back to the safe.

"Mr Goodman. Did you hear me?"

The old man opened the two doors of the safe again. Peter felt that he had lost. He got up and turned to go. He was halfway across the room when he heard Goodman closing the first door of the safe. Just before he got to the door, he heard Goodman lock the safe. Peter opened the door of the office.

"Peter. One moment!"

He turned. The old man had not put one of the stones back in the safe and was holding it out to him. Peter knew that Goodman called it the Demon King. It was the only stone in the collection that Goodman had never talked about.

"Hold this in your hand," Goodman said.

Peter took it. When he looked into it, he thought he saw a cold blue light in it.

"This stone belonged to a powerful family of Indian princes for hundreds of years. They believed that it brought victory to those who carried it in war. It brings good luck. "

Peter stared at the stone and then at the old man.

"That's why I'm giving you this stone now. Take it with you to South Africa," Goodman told him. He smiled.

Suddenly Peter felt a strange warmth from the stone. For a moment, the colour seemed to change. It became red, as if there were a brilliant fire in its centre.

Goodman pointed at the dead fly in the spider's web.

"I don't want that to happen to you," he said.

CHAPTER FOUR
Stephanie

Peter left for South Africa the next evening. He had to change planes in Amsterdam. The whole journey took fourteen hours. He did not sleep at all. When he arrived in Johannesburg, he had to take another plane to Bloemfontein, about an hour away.

A tall, slim young woman with long, brown hair and very blue eyes was waiting for him at the airport. It was Stephanie. He could never forget those eyes.

"My car's over there," she said. She did not smile.

They walked out of the air-conditioned airport to the car park. It was like walking into a very hot oven.

"Where are we going exactly?" he asked.

"To our house. You can stay there. Or did you want to stay in a hotel?"

"No, your house is all right. But where is it?"

"Near Kimberley. Get in. I'll show you the mine first."

He was so tired that he almost fell asleep in the seat next to her as she drove, but then she began talking about her father.

"I think he found out something. Something they didn't want him to know."

"They? Who exactly do you mean?"

She looked at him as if he were a stupid child.

"Bonington and Hartwell, of course. Weren't you listening?"

Peter was angry but he tried not to show it.

"Yes, of course I was listening. I just want to make sure that I understood everything. So tell me again what your father said."

"He phoned me when I was in Cape Town. He said he had

heard Bonington and Hartwell arguing. He didn't really want to talk about it on the phone. He said he'd tell me more when I came home for the weekend. And then, the next day, he disappeared."

"What do you think really happened to your father?"

"I don't know. But I don't believe he was kidnapped by terrorists."

"Do you think he's d –," he began, and then stopped.

She looked at him quickly. She was driving very fast, and she overtook the sports car in front of them.

"Do I think he's dead? Is that what you wanted to asked me?"

"Yes."

She thought for several seconds before she answered.

"No, I don't think they've killed him. Not yet."

He suddenly noticed her hands. They looked very strong. He remembered someone saying that she was a gymnast.

"Why do you think he isn't dead?" he asked.

She gave him a sharp angry look. He began to feel very nervous. She was like a bomb waiting to explode.

"Because the police haven't found his body, of course. They could easily kill him and make it look like an accident. But they haven't done that. So Bonington and Hartwell still need him."

"Need him? Need him for what?"

"Nobody will believe that terrorists kidnapped my father without a reason. And the only reason terrorists would do such a thing is for money. That's why Bonington has to keep my father alive for a while."

He looked at the countryside around them. It was flat and very dry under the hot, red sun. They were driving towards some blue hills. He stared at the road ahead. Stephanie was overtaking a big lorry. Some cars were coming towards them very fast. Stephanie was still talking.

"Bonington will pretend that he's trying to deal with the terrorists for a few more days. Then he'll kill my father and say the terrorists did it because their demands were not met. Can't you see that?"

She overtook the lorry just in time.
Two cars rushed past them from the
opposite direction. Peter tried to speak
calmly.

"Won't he try to kill you, too? How
can he be sure your father didn't tell you
what he had found out?"

"He knows I've been away in Cape Town. He
doesn't know that I spoke to my father on the phone
every evening."

The hills in front of them became larger.
They drove down into a valley. Everything in the
valley was covered by a strange blue rock.

Peter knew that diamonds came from the rock.
It was taken from the mines below the earth and
left in the sun for two years. After that, the rock
was crushed and the diamonds were extracted
from it. He had known all that before he came
to South Africa, but he had not known or
been able to imagine what the land itself really
looked like under this heavy blanket of
crushed stone. It was like pictures of the
surface of the moon – everything was blue
and everything was dead.

She stopped the car and
they got out. Stephanie
pointed to a large,
ten-storey building.

"That's the Bonington Mine there. Eric Bonington's office is on the sixth floor of that tall building. Hartwell's office is there, too, but his laboratory is below ground level."

There were a few trees next to the building, and they were the only green things in the whole valley.

"It's ugly, isn't it? My father said that he wanted to make it beautiful again," Stephanie said, looking around the valley.

"How?"

"By planting more trees. He said he could remember what it was like when he was a young man. There were some mines here at that time, too, but the land around the mines was green. He saw antelope and other wild animals grazing here when he was a boy. He even saw some wild elephants once."

"Where do you think they could be keeping your father?" he asked quietly.

"I don't know. But I have an idea he's in one of the mines, perhaps under the laboratory."

"How many mines are there?"

"Two. Part of Hartwell's laboratory is just above Number One mine. That mine was closed a few years ago. Number Two mine isn't far away. It's just on the other side of the building. There are tunnels from the building into both mines. Number Two mine is deeper than Number One and it's on the other side of the building. Those tunnels are important."

"Important? How? In what way?"

"I'll tell you later."

Peter thought for a moment. Perhaps Stephanie had some kind of plan but didn't want to tell him about it. He tried to remember all the other things she had told him so far.

"Tell me again about the argument your father heard last week."

"He was working late in the office. He thought he was alone in the building. He didn't work so late very often, but that evening he had to finish a report. Anyway, he heard a noise on the floor above. Nobody else was supposed to be there. So he went upstairs. He could hear Bonington and Hartwell talking about the technical process of making synthetic gemstone diamonds. Hartwell said there were still problems with it and that he needed more time."

"Really? But the newspapers say the process is already perfect."

"Of course that's what the newspapers say. They believe what Bonington says about the process. But he was lying – and he also knew that my father had heard him arguing with Hartwell."

"How did he know that?"

"He probably heard my father's footsteps. He came out of the office and found my father standing there. My father pretended he had just come and that he hadn't heard anything…"

She made a sudden movement, like a wild animal in a cage.

"Oh, let's go home," she said.

They turned back to her car.

"I'd like to see that machine Hartwell uses," he said.

"The one in the laboratory? The one he says he can use to make diamonds?

"Yes."

Stephanie said nothing. They got into the car. She started

the engine and they drove back to the town. After about twenty minutes they came to a pleasant, large house with a garden around it. The sun was high in the sky but the house was cool in the shadows of the trees and bushes. They went into a room with a large window next to a swimming pool. Peter sat down on a sofa. Stephanie was looking at him again, with the same look as before. Her electric blue eyes made him feel very uncomfortable.

"You're very tired, aren't you? Why don't you lie down here and get some sleep?" she said.

He lay down on the sofa. She was right. He was very tired. His eyes began to close.

"I'm going out again. I'll be back later," he heard her say.

He sat up.

"But where are you going?"

She was still looking at him with those electric blue eyes of hers.

"I'll explain later. Get some rest. You need it," she said.

He wanted to ask her something else but couldn't remember what. He lay down on the sofa again and fell asleep almost immediately.

✧ ✧ ✧ ✧

He dreamt that he was falling. Falling into a dark hole. As he fell into the hole, he saw a spider's web. He was a small insect and the spider was waiting for him.

"No!" he shouted.

He felt a strong hand shaking him. He woke up. He looked down and saw Stephanie's long, firm fingers. They were around his wrist.

"What's wrong?" he asked. He was still on the sofa but it was dark outside. He looked at his watch. It was nine o'clock.

"I came back only a few minutes ago. I heard you shouting. You were dreaming," she said.

She had some papers in her hand. They were drawings. They looked like technical drawings.

He was very thirsty.

"Have you got any water?"

She put the drawings on a table next to him and walked towards the kitchen.

"Where have you been?" he asked.

He looked quickly at the papers on the table and saw that they were the plans of Hartwell's laboratory. She came back from the kitchen.

"In Hartwell's office," she said very quietly, and gave him a glass of cold water.

"What? Did you say 'in Hartwell's office?'"

"Yes. Drink the water. Some coffee will be ready soon."

"Coffee?"

"Yes. You'll need it... I'm going down the mine tonight. You'll have to wake up if you want to come with me."

He drank the water, but there was fear in his eyes. He stared at her.

"Come with you? Down the mine, you mean?"

"Yes. Didn't you say you wanted to see Hartwell's machine? Well, it's below ground, in Hartwell's laboratory, and the only way into the laboratory is though the old mine."

He wanted to tell her how much he hated going below ground. He opened his mouth, but he couldn't find the words. She looked at him.

"You aren't afraid, are you?"

He said nothing for a moment.

"But how will you... I mean... we get into the mine?"

"I used to play in the valley when I was a child. There was an old tunnel. It goes down into the old mine. I found the tunnel again. It's a little dangerous. But as I said, it's the only way you can get into the laboratory. Don't be afraid. You can trust me," she said quietly. She was looking at the plans again.

"As the spider said to the fly," he said suddenly.

"What?"

She looked at him in surprise.

He didn't answer. For a moment he wondered if he was still dreaming.

CHAPTER FIVE

In the spider's web

The smell of fresh, hot coffee filled the air. Stephanie got up and went back into the kitchen.

"You still haven't told me how I can get into the laboratory," Peter said when she came back. She handed him a cup of coffee and began drinking from another cup. Then she pointed to the drawings.

"These are the plans of Hartwell's laboratory. It gets very hot there. That's why it's air-conditioned. Look. The cool air comes into the laboratory through a large pipe or shaft. Part of the shaft comes down into the mine."

He drank the coffee and looked at the drawing. His head began to feel clearer.

"Where did you get these plans?"

"From Hartwell's office. I told you."

"But how did you get into the his office?"

"It was dark. And there are some trees at the side of the main building."

She looked at him carefully. Then she suddenly smiled. Peter remembered seeing the trees earlier that day. He also remembered that they were close to the building... but not that close. Then he also remembered that Stephanie was a gymnast. He looked down at the plans again.

"Are you saying we can get into the laboratory through the air conditioning shaft?"

"Yes. Exactly."

"But how do you know we can get into the shaft through the mine?"

She smiled at him again.

"Finish your coffee. Then come with me and find out."

He drank the rest of the coffee. His hand was shaking. He hoped she didn't notice.

They drove towards the valley. Peter could feel his heart beating fast. His fear of being below the ground had started when he was very young. His interest in diamonds had something to do with this fear. He remembered the first time he had seen a diamond catch the light and reflect it brilliantly. When he was younger it had been a great mystery to him. How could these things glow and sparkle? They had been for so long deep in the dark earth, away from the light and sun. He shivered, although the night was still warm.

Stephanie parked the car. They got out and walked down into the valley. She was dressed all in black. Even in the moonlight he could hardly see her. They came to a tunnel in the upper part of the valley. It was very dark here. They went into the tunnel. Stephanie was just in front of him. She carried a bag across her shoulder. She pulled out a small electric torch.

"There's a hole in the tunnel wall in front. I'll go through first," she said. She turned her head back towards him when she spoke. He could feel her warm breath on his face.

The hole was very narrow. Somehow she got through it. Then she put her hand out from the other side.

"Come on," she whispered.

She took his hand and began to pull him through the hole. He was surprised how strong she was. Suddenly some of the earth above him fell down. Stephanie stopped pulling.

"What have I got myself into here?" he thought. He remembered the spider's web in the dream again.

"Don't move," she whispered. They were both quiet for a moment. The earth stopped falling.

"One more try now," she said and began pulling him again. Suddenly he was through the hole. He straightened up in the darkness.

"I can't see anything? Where are we?"

"This is the main part of the mine. Just follow me. Don't be afraid," she answered.

"As the spider said to the fly," he wanted to say again. But he didn't.

They crawled a long way through the mine and then up another tunnel. Suddenly they heard the sound of metal. Stephanie pointed the light from her torch onto a large screen. It was made of wire.

"We're at the bottom of the air conditioning shaft. Some of the warm air is blown back into the mine. All Hartwell's machines are on the other side of this screen."

He looked through the screen. He could see some lights in the darkness. They looked like the lights on the dials and controls of machines.

"But how are we going to get though the screen?"

"With these," she said, and took a pair of wire cutters from her bag.

He held the torch and she began cutting a square piece of wire away from the screen. It made a hole that was just large enough for him to get through. As he climbed through it, he felt a sharp pain. He had cut his cheek on the end of one of wires. "Ouch!" he said, as he dropped to the floor of the laboratory.

"What's wrong? Are you all right?"

"Yes."

"I'll be back in exactly thirty minutes," she whispered and gave him another small electric torch from the bag. Then she turned and went back through the hole in the screen again.

The light from the torch was just strong enough for Peter to see the machines in the laboratory. The biggest one was in the centre of the room. There was a large steel desk in front of it, and there were lots of dials, switches and other controls on it. The machine was very similar to one he had seen at the General Electric Company in New York. But that machine made only small diamonds, not real gemstones.

The cut on his face was still painful but he tried to forget about it. He looked at the big machine very carefully. One of the dials measured the heat inside the machine. He looked at the highest measurement. Then he looked at the dial that

showed the highest possible air pressure inside the machine. He pulled a small notebook out of his back pocket and wrote down the figures.

The time passed very quickly. There was a sound behind him. It was Stephanie.

She was in the shaft on the other side of the screen. In the darkness he could see only her white face and her eyes. She held out her hand and helped him to climb up and through the screen again. Again, he was surprised how strong she was.

"What did you find in the mine?" he asked.

"I'll tell you later. First help me with this," she said, and pointed at the piece of wire she had cut from the screen. She took some heavy black tape from the bag. He held the piece of wire she had cut. She taped the ends of it back on to the screen. Soon there was no hole any more.

"Nobody will realise we've been here, unless they look at that screen very carefully," she said.

They crawled back through the tunnel for twenty minutes. Finally they came back up into the valley again. In the moonlight, it looked even more strange and unfriendly. They walked to the car. Before they got into it, Stephanie looked back. The valley was silent.

When they got back to her house, it was almost three o'clock in the morning. Peter took a shower. As the hot water washed the dirt away, he remembered the cut on his face. The bleeding had stopped, but the cut was deeper than he had thought. He put on some clean clothes and then went into the kitchen. Stephanie was making some more coffee. She had taken a shower and changed clothes, too.

"So, what did you think of Hartwell's laboratory?" she asked.

He told her about the machine he had examined.

"Do you really think he can make diamonds with it?" she asked.

Peter thought carefully before he answered.

"Yes, but only small ones. Not diamonds of gemstone quality. I saw a machine almost exactly like it in New York a few months ago. I talked to the engineers there who developed it. They think it will take a long time to solve the problems of making artificial gemstones. Those people in New York are the best engineers in the world. Perhaps Hartwell knows something they don't know... but I don't think so."

"I see," said Stephanie, as she poured the coffee.

"You know Hartwell. What do you think of him?" Peter asked her.

"He's weak. Very weak. Bonington has complete control over him."

"And how well do you know Bonington?"

"Not very well. I don't think anyone knows him very well. He's a mystery – even to people like my father who have worked for him for years."

Stephanie looked at the cut on Peter's face and went to get something to put on it. When she came back, she had a box of plasters and a bottle with some dark red liquid in it.

"This won't hurt much. Just stay still," she said.

When she put the red liquid on the cut, he suddenly felt a sharp, burning pain in his cheek.

"What *is* that stuff?" he shouted.

"Iodine, of course. I just want to make sure the cut doesn't become infected."

Peter screwed up his face, and Stephanie put a small plaster over the cut.

"Why do you say that Bonington has complete control over Hartwell?" he asked when the burning feeling became less painful.

"Because even when Hartwell knows he's right, Bonington always wins the argument."

Her bright blue eyes seemed to become even larger when she spoke. When Peter looked at them it was difficult for him to listen to her words.

"What do you mean 'Bonington always wins the argument?' How?"

"When Hartwell says he wants some kind of new machine for his laboratory, Bonington always says there isn't enough

Savas

money to buy it. Don't you remember the argument my father heard? Hartwell never gets what he wants from Bonington. He's too weak."

Peter thought about this for a moment. A machine that could really make diamonds would cost a tremendous amount of money. How could Hartwell possibly develop such a machine if he didn't have enough money? However, Peter knew that scientists always said they needed more money. Was it possible that Hartwell could never be satisfied? Were his arguments with Bonington like the arguments most scientists had with their financial directors?

He was beginning to feel very tired again. He began to yawn, and he put his hand in front of his mouth.

"What did you find in the mine when I was in the laboratory?" he asked.

"Another tunnel. I'll tell you about it in the morning."

Once again he had the feeling that there was something she didn't want to tell him. What could it be? Then he thought of the dark mine and all its even darker tunnels. He never wanted to go down a mine again. Never!

He yawned again. It was late.

"You have an appointment with Bonington tomorrow afternoon. What are you going to ask him?" Stephanie asked.

"That's a good question."

"Well, what's the answer?"

"I wish I knew," Peter said.

39

CHAPTER SIX
The meeting with Bonington

"I'm afraid Mr Bonington will be a few minutes late. Won't you take a seat? " the receptionist said. Peter sat down. He suddenly felt cold. It was so warm outside, but so cool inside the building. A few minutes went by.

"You're lucky your appointment wasn't for this morning," the receptionist said.

Peter looked at her.

"Why?"

"Because there was something wrong with the air conditioning system here and in the other building. The technicians have just left. Thank heavens it's working again. It was terribly hot in here this morning."

Just then the outer door of the office opened. The man who came in was about sixty. He was wearing a light blue suit. It looked very expensive.

"Mr Rogers? Peter Rogers?" he asked.

"Yes. You must be Eric Bonington."

Eric Bonington was not a very big man. His face was thin. There were dark shadows under his eyes.

"Sorry to have kept you waiting. Please come to my office."

Peter walked into a big room with a very large desk. The walls seem to be full of eyes and heads. They were the heads of animals – antelope, buffalo – even a lion. Below each head there was a small metal plate with information about the date and place each animal had been killed and the kind of rifle that had been used.

"Have a seat," Bonington said. He pointed to a chair covered in a zebra skin. Peter sat down. Bonington sat down, too, just below the head of the dead lion. The glass eyes of the lion were staring directly at Peter. He moved around in his chair uncomfortably.

Bonington asked him how he was and about the flight from London.

"And how's my old friend in London, David Goodman?"

"Oh, he's fine," Peter answered.

"And how's business?" Bonington asked.

Peter looked at the eyes of the lion again and than at Bonington again. Why did he feel so uncomfortable with Bonington?

"Not bad. Not bad at all."

"Glad to hear it," Bonington said and looked at his watch.

"Now, what can I do for you, Mr Rogers? Why have you come all this way?"

Peter took a deep breath.

"Well, I had two reasons. First of all I came because of Stephanie's father. I met him and Stephanie when they were in London last year and I thought that perhaps I could help in some way."

Bonington frowned.

"Help in some way? How?"

"Well, I'm not sure. I mean... well..."

Bonington looked at his watch again.

"There's nothing you can do that we aren't already doing, Mr Rogers. Believe me. Now you said you had two reasons for coming. What was the other reason?"

"Well, I'm very interested in this new technical process of yours. You say you can make diamonds of gemstone quality with it."

"No, I don't say that. Professor Hartwell says it. He's a very respected scientist and I believe him."

"Do you think I could talk to Professor Hartwell?" Peter asked.

Bonington frowned again.

"Talk to him? Why?"

"Because... because he's the inventor of the process, and naturally I thought he could give me information about the process that nobody else can."

"The information is very technical. Are you a scientist, Mr Rogers?"

"No, but I know something about these things and... well, I thought..."

"Professor Hartwell is going to give a press conference tomorrow. You can ask him any questions you want then," Bonington said.

Suddenly the telephone rang. Bonington picked it up.

"Yes, what is it?"

Bonington listened to the person on the other end of the telephone. Then he stared at Peter for a moment. He was looking at the plaster on his cheek.

"What? Are you sure?" he said.

Bonington put the phone down. He seemed to be thinking. The silence in the office was broken only by the sound of the air conditioning. Peter looked up at the wall again and at the head of the lion. Suddenly he realised why he felt so uncomfortable with Bonington. The look in the older man's eyes was like the lion's eyes. It was dead and glassy.

"How did that happen?" Bonington suddenly asked, and pointed at the plaster on Peter's cheek.

"Oh, it's only a cut."

"A cut? Have you seen a doctor about it?"

"No. It's nothing serious."

Bonington suddenly stood up. So did Peter. The two men began walking towards the door.

"By the way, where are you staying? Which hotel?" Bonington asked.

"As it happens, I'm staying with... well, with Stephanie. I mean, I'm staying in her house."

"When did she come back from Cape Town?"

"I'm not sure. I think she came back as soon as she heard that her father had been kidnapped. Why?"

"Nothing."

They were almost at the door. Bonington stopped and looked at Peter.

"Would you like to see our new cutting machines?" he asked.

"Cutting machines?"

"Yes. They're much faster than the older ones. Perhaps you'd like to see them."

"Yes. That would be, er... very interesting. When?"

"Let's do it now," Bonington said.

He did not wait for an answer. He took Peter by the arm and led him past his secretary in the outer office and through the glass door to the lift.

"Wait here for a moment. I'll be right back," Bonington said suddenly.

The older man went back through the glass door and said something to his secretary. Then he picked up the phone and spoke to someone else. Peter saw his lips moving but couldn't hear what he was saying. Then Bonington went back into his own office. He came out again after about a minute. Peter was standing in front of the lift that he had used earlier.

"No, not this lift. Come this way," Bonington said and took Peter down a dark corridor. They walked past some large wooden boxes and came to another lift. Bonington opened the heavy metal door of the lift.

"You first," he said.

Peter looked inside. He could see that the lift was used for equipment and other things. There was only one rather weak light bulb in it. He hesitated before he walked in.

"Where are we going?" he asked.

"To see the new cutting machines. I told you."

"Yes, but where exactly are they?"

"In the mine, of course. Where else?" Bonington answered.

He shut the heavy door behind them with a loud bang. Peter felt his heart beating faster again. He wanted to turn and rush out of the lift but it was too late. They had already started going down.

The lift went past the ground floor without stopping. They continued going down. Peter wondered how far below the surface they were. Finally the lift stopped. Bonington opened the door. Another man was standing there. He was very big and he was wearing a helmet. He was holding another

helmet and some dark blue work-clothes.

"This is Michael," Bonington said.

The big man stared at Peter coldly, without smiling. He handed him the helmet, the work-clothes and a mask.

"Put this on. Go in there," he said, and pointed to a door.

Peter went through the door into a small room with a metal cabinet, a wash-basin and a toilet. He took off his own clothes and put them in the cabinet. Then he put on the work-clothes. The helmet was far too big for him. When he came out, Michael was putting something in his pocket. Peter couldn't see what it was.

"Michael will take good care of you," Bonington told Peter. He went back into the lift, leaving Peter alone with Michael.

"We go this way. Put the mask over your face," Michael said and pointed down a long, wide corridor. There were only a few lights hanging from the ceiling. Peter felt like a man on his way to the electric chair. Michael was just behind him. The air was full of dust.

From the other end of the corridor, Peter could hear the sound of heavy metal, of breaking and cutting. It became louder with each step they took. Dark men with helmets and masks pushed metal wagons past them. The noise and heat were terrible. At the end of the corridor they came to two tunnels. The one on the right was wide. The one on the left was narrow. The big man pointed to the wide tunnel.

"This tunnel goes to Number Two mine."

Then he pointed to the narrow tunnel on the left.

"But we go down this one."

He said the words like a command.

It was even hotter in the narrow tunnel and the air was filled with dust. Peter hit his head on some heavy rock hanging from the ceiling. The big helmet almost fell off.

"What's wrong?" Michael shouted.

"This helmet. It's too big for me"

The big man took the helmet off Peter's head. There were some straps inside.

"I will make the straps tighter for you later. Go on," he said.

Peter went a few more metres down the tunnel. It became darker. He knew Michael was behind him, but didn't know exactly where. He put his hand out, trying to touch the wall of the tunnel. He wasn't sure what happened then, but suddenly he fell. There was an explosion of pain in his head. Everything went black.

When he woke up, he was alone in the narrow tunnel.

"What happened? Where am I?" he asked himself.

He tried to get to his feet, but couldn't. His head hurt very badly. He sat with his back to the wall of the tunnel. He tore the mask off his face but there was so much dust in the air that he choked when he breathed. Somewhere in the distance he thought he heard voices.

"Help!" he shouted.

He choked again, and put the mask back on. The voices seemed to be nearer. He opened his eyes and saw Michael and two other men. The other men were carrying a stretcher. One of the men took Peter by the arms. The other man took him by the legs. They lifted Peter on to the stretcher. Everything went black again.

When Peter woke up again, he was lying in a small room. A nurse was looking at him.

"You hit your head, but it's not serious. I've given you something. It will make you sleep," the nurse said.

Peter slept. When he opened his eyes again, he saw his clothes hanging next to the bed. A piece of paper was sticking out of the pocket of his jacket. The paper was torn and dirty. Part of a poem was printed on it.

"Stars and darkness,
Sound and silence,
Lightening and clouds appear
And then disappear again
Like echoes in a dream."

Just below these words, someone had written a few more words in pencil.

Deep down. Probably the dead well.

Peter stared at the strange words. What did they mean? The nurse came back.

"Stephanie Powers is here. She will drive you to her home. You will be more comfortable there," she said.

Peter put the paper back in his jacket.

CHAPTER SEVEN

The dead well

Stephanie drove Peter home. He told her what had happened in the mine. Suddenly he remembered the piece of paper. He found it in his pocket and showed it to her.

"Have you any idea what this is?" he asked.

She stared at it.

"It's part of a longer poem. It comes from one of my father's favourite books. He probably had the book with him the day he disappeared. Where did you get it?"

He explained how he had found it in his pocket.

"What do you mean you 'found' it?"

"All I know is that it wasn't in my pocket before. Some workmen carried me out of the mine. Perhaps one of them put it in my pocket."

She looked at the page again.

"This looks like my father's handwriting. But the paper is so torn and the words are so badly written that it's hard to tell."

She stared at the words written in pencil.

"What's this about a dead well?" she said.

She began studying the plans of the mine again.

"I remember my father saying something about a dead well. They found it a few years ago when they built a new part of the main building . There's no water in it any more. That's why they called it the dead well."

She showed him the plans of the two mines and the building on top of them. There were only two lifts in the building.

"This is probably where I was earlier today," he said, pointing to a tunnel in the drawing.

"Really? The bottom of the dead well is just on the other

side of the tunnel. Do you think you could find that tunnel again?"

"Yes, I think so."

"Good. You can show me where it is when we go down again."

Peter hoped he hadn't heard her correctly. All his life he had been afraid of going underground. Now in less than twenty-four hours he had been down a mine twice. Did she really expect him to go down a third time? He put his hands over his eyes.

"What's wrong?" she asked.

"Are you really serious?"

"About what?"

"About going down the mine again."

"Of course I am. I have to find out if my father's really down there."

He tried not to look at her eyes. They had a strange power over him.

"But what if this is all part of Bonington's plan? Perhaps Bonington told someone to put that page in my pocket. Perhaps he wants us to go down the mine so that he can kill us," he shouted.

She turned away from him and walked over to the window. The sun was just setting. She looked at it for a minute or more without saying anything. Then she turned back to him.

"Yes, it could all be part of Bonington's plan. But perhaps it isn't. All I know is that I have to go down and look for my father," she said slowly.

His heart sank and he listened to her. He hated the thought of going down the mine again.

"But what about the security guards? They're in front of all the entrances to the main building. How will it be possible to get past them?" he asked.

She thought for a moment.

"Hartwell is going to give a press conference tomorrow morning. Perhaps we can get in then," she suddenly said.

"But how? What's the press conference got to with it?"

"I'll explain later. Just tell me one thing. Will you come with me? Will you help me, Peter?"

She was looking directly at him again. He could not avoid her eyes.

"I know it's dangerous, but it's our only chance of finding my father before it's too late."

Her voice was softer, as she spoke. The colour of her large blue eyes had become deeper and warmer. He thought of the Demon King diamond in his pocket and how the colour had changed when he held it. Suddenly he knew that he had to go down the mine again with her.

He went upstairs to the spare bedroom. He could hear her telephoning in the room below. She was very busy, making plans. He tried not to think about the mine and the darkness in it. His eyes closed. He fell asleep.

✧ ✧ ✧ ✧

In the cold light of the early morning he took a long, hot shower and then went downstairs to the kitchen. Stephanie was making coffee there again. They had breakfast in silence. It was almost seven o'clock.

"We have to be in the hills above the mine at 7.30," she said.

"Why?"

"We're going to meet someone," she said and drank some more coffee.

"Who?"

"Just come with me and see."

Before they left, he went back to the room he had slept in. The Demon King was on the table next to the bed. He picked it up. It felt warm. He remembered Goodman's words in London. "It brings good luck," the old man had said.

✧ ✧ ✧ ✧

At 7.30 they were above the valley, on the hill road. A large van was coming towards them.

"Do you know anything about TV cameras?" Stephanie asked Peter.

"No, absolutely nothing."

"Well, perhaps you can learn quickly. You're going to be a TV cameraman this morning."

The lorry stopped in front of them. A tall fair-haired man was sitting next to the driver. He smiled at Stephanie.

"Hello, Piet," she said and spoke to him quickly in Afrikaans. She and Peter got into the back of the van. There were three other men there. They smiled and nodded at Stephanie.

"What do I have to do with this stuff?" Peter asked. He pointed at the camera cases.

"Just carry them into the building – *ja*. We'll do the rest," one of the men said, and laughed.

Stephanie gave Peter some sunglasses and a loose cap which almost hid his face.

The van stopped. They were in front of the main entrance to the building. The security guards let them go into the building with the television cameras. Peter and Stephanie carried camera cases down into the laboratory. A tall, heavy man in a white jacket was standing nervously in front of the biggest machine there. He turned around as Peter and Stephanie came in.

"Stephanie... is it you?"

His voice was strangely high and soft. It was like a girl's voice.

"Hello, Professor Hartwell," Stephanie said.

"What are you doing here?"

"I"m working with the local TV station in Bloemfontein."

"Really... but... but I thought you were studying chemistry at Cape Town University."

"Yes. I was. But I gave up my studies. I want to work in television. This is very good experience," she told him.

Hartwell stared at her.

"I'm sorry, Professor Hartwell, but I have a lot of work to do," she said with a smile.

She and Peter went back up to ground level.

"Wait here," she told Peter. She went past the security guards at the entrance and walked to the van. When she came back, she was carrying a large bag. Then they went through a door and down another corridor. They passed empty offices. They found the second lift.

"What happens if someone sees us when we get into the tunnels?" Peter asked as they got into the lift.

"That's why I brought this bag with me," she said.

She opened it. It was full of miners' work-clothes. There were also two helmets in the bag.

"Put these things on. Hurry!" she said.

When they got out of the lift at the bottom of the shaft, they were both dressed like mine-workers. They began walking down the corridor. The dust, noise and heat were just as bad as before. A few men passed them, but they did not even look at Peter or Stephanie. Nobody spoke to them. They walked quickly, their faces half-hidden by their helmets.

They came to the place where two tunnels crossed. They could hear the noise of machines at the end of the tunnel on the left.

"When I was here yesterday, we went down the tunnel on the right," Peter said.

Stephanie had brought the plan of the mine with her. She studied it for a moment.

"This the way to dead well," she said.

They went down the first tunnel and then into another one. This one was not as well-lit as the first. They walked for ten or fifteen minutes. The noise of the machines seemed far away. They found a third tunnel. It was very dark. The only light came from Stephanie's electric torch. As they walked on, they could hear only their own footsteps and the sound of their own breathing.

Then they saw a large machine in front of them.

"This must be the new cutting machine Bonington told me about," Peter said.

The machine had a large drill in front. The drill could move up or down and to the left and right. Someone had used it to cut a square out of the dark blue rock. The square was almost the size of a small room. It was about two metres high and two metres wide. The drill had also cut a small hole in the wall in front of them. Stephanie shone the torch through the hole and leaned forward to see better.

She stayed like that for a moment. Then she turned round.

"I can't see much but I think it's the bottom of the dead well," she said.

Before Peter could stop her, she climbed up and crawled right through the hole. Peter followed her through the hole and into the well. It was surprisingly big. It looked more like a large cave than the bottom of a well.

In the light from Stephanie's torch, they saw that the rock around them here was much lighter than the dark blue rock on the other side of the hole.

"It looks like sandstone or something," Peter said.

Stephanie turned her torch upwards. There was nothing above their heads, only darkness.

Suddenly they heard a strange sound from the far corner of the well. They climbed over some loose rocks and looked down. In the weak light from Stephanie's torch, they saw a man. His hands and legs were tied, and there was something over his mouth. Stephanie pointed the light down at his face.

"It's him! It's my father!" she shouted.

Her voice echoed all around them.

"Is he alive?" Peter asked.

Just then Peter heard another, much louder noise. It came from the other side of the hole they had crawled through. Peter saw a man there. It was Michael, the man who had been with Peter the day before. Michael started the engine of the cutting machine and drove the drill up into the blue rock just on the other side of the hole. Heavy pieces of the dark blue rock began to crash down.

Peter could see that in a few moments the blue rock would completely cover the hole. He, Stephanie and her father would never get out. They would die there. Somehow he had to stop Michael.

Peter got his head through the hole, but the rest of his body was still in the well. Michael pointed the drill at Peter and drove the machine forward. The drill came very close but cut into the rock instead. Peter pushed himself out of the

well and fell in front of the machine. A piece of dark blue
rock fell at the same time and almost hit him. Peter rolled to
the side and got to his feet. Then Michael drove the machine
towards him again. Peter jumped out of the way but the
machine hit him. He fell to the floor and did not move.

Michael pointed the drill at the ceiling of dark blue rock
above the hole. More heavy pieces fell in front of it.

CHAPTER EIGHT
The press conference

Peter lay on the floor for several seconds without moving. Michael had driven the machine past him and was drilling into the rock outside the well. Blue dust filled the air in the tunnel.

Peter felt a sudden, sharp shock in his left side. What was it? He rolled over. He could feel the Demon King diamond in his left pocket. Then he felt a second shock. It came from the Demon King! Peter took the diamond out of his pocket and got to his feet. He felt a rush of strength go through his whole body. Just in front of him, he saw Michael driving the cutting machine through the blue dust.

The Demon King began to feel warm and heavy in his hand. Peter aimed the diamond at Michael and threw it as hard as he could. Michael was wearing a helmet but the stone hit him just below it, on the back of his neck. The big man fell forward on top of the machine controls. The engine stopped.

The drill was no longer turning. Peter ran past it. He pulled heavy pieces of rock away from the hole which led into the well.

Inside the well Stephanie was looking down at her father. He was moving his lips, trying to say something.

Peter was still on the other side. He pulled Michael off the seat of the machine and started the engine again. Then he began to drill a much bigger hole into the wall of the well.

Stephanie's father moved his lips again.

"Water. Quick, please give me some water."

Stephanie could hear the sound of the drill outside. The wall of the well began to shake. Suddenly pieces of the light grey rock crashed down next to the dark blue rock outside the wall. The hole was much bigger. Peter came through it.

Stephanie and Peter carried her father out of the well. They put him down, next to Michael.

"Turn Michael over," Stephanie said.

The big man was lying on his back. Peter rolled him over.

"Look at his belt. Miners always carry some water with them," she explained.

Peter saw a round metal bottle hanging from the belt. He took it and gave it to Stephanie.

She held the bottle to her father's lips. He began to drink.

"We must get him up to the company hospital," she said.

Professor Hartwell smiled into the television camera. Bonington was sitting on his left. Hartwell began speaking in his high voice.

"Now, ladies and gentlemen, as I said earlier, with my new process, it is possible to make synthetic gemstones of the highest quality. Let me explain."

Hartwell pointed to the table in front of him. There was a piece of dark blue rock on the table, and some pieces of dark grey rock. The camera focused on them. Hartwell picked up the blue rock first.

"This is kimberlite, the rock we get gemstone diamonds from. Thousands, perhaps millions of years ago, this rock came under enormous heat and pressure." Hartwell put the blue rock down pushed his two hands together to show the idea of pressure. Then he picked up the grey rocks.

"I shall now demonstrate to you how my machine can use that same heat and pressure on these pieces of graphite, to produce top quality diamonds..."

Not very far away, in the company hospital, Peter and Stephanie were sitting in the visitors' room. They were watching Hartwell on the television screen.

A nurse came out of the smaller room next door and walked over to them. It was the same nurse Peter had spoken to the afternoon before.

"Your father will be all right, Miss Powers. But he is very weak. He wants to see you," she said.

Stephanie left the visitors' room. Peter looked at the television screen again. it now showed a large machine – the one that Peter had seen in Hartwell's laboratory.

"Exactly how much pressure does your machine produce?" a reporter asked.

"I'm afraid the scientific details of my process must be a secret. I'm sure you understand. There are thousands of companies interested in it," Hartwell said with a smile. He looked at his watch and turned to the machine.

"Do you see this red light? When it goes off in a few minutes, I will open the oven. You all saw me put the graphite in the oven half an hour ago. When I open the oven, you will see ten uncut diamonds, each of about five carats."

At that moment, Stephanie came back from her father's room.

"My father wants to thank you, Peter," she said.

She took Peter into the next room. Mr Powers was lying in a bed. He looked pale and ill but his eyes were open. He took Peter's hand.

"You saved my life. You saved Stephanie's life," he said in a weak voice.

"No, the Demon King saved all our lives, sir," Peter said.

Mr Powers did not understand.

"What? The Demon King?"

"Yes. It's a diamond. I wonder if Professor Hartwell can make one like it with his new process?"

When Mr Powers heard Hartwell's name, he tried to sit up.

"I know about Hartwell's process. There are still very serious problems with it."

"Well, Hartwell is demonstrating the process on television now. He's giving a press conference. And he's just told everybody he can produce high quality diamonds by machine. He's showing them now. "

Mr Powers could hear Hartwell's voice coming from the television in the visitors' room. He began to get out of bed. The nurse tried to stop him.

"I must watch this demonstration. Help me," he said.

When he got out of bed, he almost fell. Stephanie and Peter helped him to walk the few steps into the next room. The television camera had moved back to get a wider view. They could see Hartwell in front of the machine and Bonington, sitting to the left of the tall professor. Hartwell had his hand on the door of the oven.

"There was tremendous heat and pressure inside this oven a few minutes ago – the same as the heat and pressure deep, deep down in the earth. And you will now see what that heat and pressure has done to the rock which I put in the oven earlier," Hartwell explained.

When he opened the oven, there was a sound like the pop of a champagne bottle when the cool air from the laboratory met the hot gases from the oven. Hartwell had put on a special mask and was wearing heavy gloves. He used a metal bar to take a container from the oven. He held the container towards the television camera and then put it on a large steel table next to the machine. When he opened the container, there was another 'pop'. The camera focused on the container. Inside it, there were some diamonds, but they were very small.

"Those aren't five carat gemstones. They're industrial diamonds," Peter said.

On the television screen, Hartwell was taking off his mask and his gloves. He looked shocked. People were laughing.

"How do you explain this, Professor Hartwell?" a reporter asked.

Hartwell opened his mouth to say something and then shut it again. His face had gone very white.

Another reporter turned to Bonington.

"Mr Bonington, as the director of this company, how do you feel?"

The camera focused on Bonington. He looked very serious.

"Yes, naturally I am disappointed that the process is not successful. Luckily, however, our company still produces natural diamonds."

Stephanie's father was staring at Bonington on the television screen.

"No! We can't let him get away with this," he said.

He began to walk towards the door.

"Where are you going?" Stephanie shouted. She and the nurse tried to stop him.

"To the press conference. I know the truth. And I'm going to tell the world about Bonington."

They had to go outside the building and around to another entrance. Mr Powers was in his hospital pyjamas. Peter and Stephanie were still covered in dust from the mine. The security guard tried to stop them.

"Look at me! Look at my face. You know me. I am the financial director of this company. These people are with me. Let us through," Mr Powers told them.

His voice was still weak but his meaning was clear. The guard opened the door.

When they got to the press conference, Bonington was still answering questions. He was standing at the front of the room and did not see Peter, Stephanie and her father when they entered from the back.

"Naturally, I'm very sorry for Professor Hartwell. He's a brilliant scientist, but I told him some time ago that I was afraid this would happen," Bonington said.

Hartwell stared at him.

"What do you mean? I told you that I needed more money for this process. You never gave me enough. This is all your fault!" he shouted.

Bonington smiled slightly and looked at the reporters.

"Naturally, Professor Hartwell thinks it is my fault. I am afraid I cannot agree. I and my company have tried to help him in every way possible but..."

The smile on Bonington's face suddenly disappeared. He had just seen Stephanie's father.

"How did you..." he began.

The reporters and cameramen turned to look at Mr Powers. Stephanie and Peter were on either side of him, holding him by the arm.

"You kidnapped me and left me in the mine to die! And you did this because I know the truth about you," Mr Powers said slowly.

His voice was still weak but it was loud enough for everyone to hear. There was a moment of complete silence in the room. Then he said simply, "Ladies and gentlemen, let me give you all the facts."

The story was soon in newspapers all over the world. Bonington had been selling his shares in the company at very high prices. The price of those shares had gone up and up when Hartwell first announced his new process. Bonington knew about the problems with this process. He also knew that if the process was not a success, the price of shares in his company would go down and down. In other words, Bonington knew he could buy shares back at a much lower price. He would make a lot of money.

There was another thing too. Hartwell's process didn't belong to Hartwell. It belonged to Bonington and his company. Bonington knew that in a few years the problems with this process could probably be solved. Bonington would already be very rich after selling his shares at a high price and buying them back at a low price. But when the problems with the new process were solved, he would be even richer.

When Stephanie's father found out about all this, Bonington's men had kidnapped him. And when Peter and Stephanie started looking around, Bonington decided to get rid of them, too. Peter was right. Bonington had put the page from the book in Peter's pocket. He planned to let Stephanie, her father and Peter die in the well. Then they could say it was all a terrible accident.

But the story of the Demon King diamond stayed a secret.

Three weeks later, it was time for Peter to go back to England. Once again he was in Bloemfontein airport with Stephanie. His flight to Johannesburg was called. He turned to her.

There was a very serious look on his face.

"There's something I should tell you. As you know, your father is the head of the company now that Bonington is in prison. And as you also know, he wants to create a nature park in the valley. Well, he's asked me to come back and work for him."

"Are you going to accept the job?" she asked.

"It depends."

"On what?"

"On you."

"On me?"

"Yes, on you. Do you want me to accept it?"

"What do you think?" she said.

Suddenly she smiled. He smiled, too.

The story you have just read takes place in the 1960s. In 1970, two scientists in America succeeded in making diamonds of gemstone quality. Today, almost half of the world's diamonds are man-made, but the price of natural diamonds has not fallen. People continue to buy them and to admire their wonderful natural qualities.

READING ACTIVITIES

Before reading

1 Look at the title of the story and the picture on the front
cover. What type of story do you think this might be?

science fiction   romance
spy story   crime

2 Read the information about the story on the back cover.
Where does it take place? What do you think Peter Rogers'
job could be?

3 Match the beginnings of these sentences (A) to their correct
endings (B). They are all facts about diamonds which will be
useful as you read the story.

A
Diamonds are found
The weight of a diamond is recorded
The largest rough diamond ever found
Diamonds are not always white,
Although diamonds can break,
Less than 20 per cent of mined diamonds
Diamonds are used in industry
If they are made by machine,

B
was the Cullinan diamond.
are of gemstone quality.
to make strong drills that will go through rock.
they are the hardest thing in nature.
diamonds are called 'synthetic'.
in South Africa, India, Brazil and Russia.
they can be yellow, blue or other colours.
in carats.

While reading

As you read the story, answer these question.

Chapters 1–2

1 Who said this?
   "It will be a disaster for companies like us."
   What was the speaker thinking about?

2 Does the phone call from South Africa bring good news or
   bad? What do you think the news might be?

Chapters 3–4

3 These sentences all contain some wrong information about
   the story. Rewrite them so that they are correct.
   a) Mr Goodman gave Peter the Demon King to help him see
      into the future.
   b) Stephanie thought that her father had been kidnapped by
      terrorists.
   c) Peter was excited about going into the mine.

4 Which of these adjectives would you use to describe
   Stephanie? Are there any other words you would choose?
   Discuss your choice with another person.

   brave   bad-tempered
   impatient   kind
   proud   unhappy
   mysterious   clever

Chapters 5–6

5 Make a list of questions you would want to ask Eric
   Bonington, if you were Peter Rogers.

6 Put these events into the right order:

   Peter had a bad accident in the mine.
   Peter went to see Bonington.
   Bonington took him to see the cutting machine.
   Bonington asked Peter about the cut on his face.
   Bonington got a phonecall.

7 What do you think Bonington found out in the phonecall?

8 Finish these sentences:

a) Stephanie wanted to go down the mine again, because...
b) Peter took the Demon King with him, because...
c) Professor Hartwell was angry with Bonington, because...

9 Work with another person to write a newspaper headline for the Bonington story. Compare your headlines in class.

10 Imagine you are Peter Rogers. You write a letter to Mr Goodman, to tell him about the Demon King. Start your letter like this:

You have probably read all about the Bonington business in the newspapers. But the strangest part of the story is this....

After reading

1 Some people are afraid of spiders, some people are afraid of heights. What things do you fear most?

Peter was afraid to go underground. Write a short dialogue between Peter and Stephanie, in which he explains why he has this fear. How might Stephanie answer?

2 Here are two well-known sayings in English:
"Diamonds are a girl's best friend."
"Diamonds are forever."

a) What do you think these sayings mean?
b) Do you agree with them?
c) What sayings about diamonds (or other precious stones) do you have in your own language? Translate these into English and explain what they mean.

3 Professor Hartwell's process didn't work, but we now know that diamonds can be made by machine. What other things can you think of that were unknown or impossible thirty years ago? Choose one example and write a short report. Include the good or bad points about it.